MU01064499

Praise for Jim Mersereau's
Getting Along without Going Along

"*Getting Along without Going Along* is an unusual gem for believers searching for good answers to hard questions. Highly engaging. Packed with Biblical references and personal experiences. A wake up call for us all."

— Stephen E. Tate,
Founder and CEO, BCT LLC

"*Getting Along without Going Along* is a must read for Christians willing to take a correct and unapologetic stand on sexual ethics but with grace, love, and respect."

— Rev. William Beasley, Pastor,
Riceville First Baptist Church

"*Getting Along without Going Along* provides a thoughtful, Biblical analysis of the issues surrounding sexual morality in our culture. It encourages Christians to boldly and unapologetically stand on the truth of God's Word, but to do so with kindness and grace."

— Scott Lacy, D.Min.,
J.D. Pastor & Attorney

"This book is a sound, biblical resource that will help generations of Bible-believing Christians answer difficult questions on sexual ethics. As followers of Jesus, we are commanded to love as He loves and serve others as He serves. A well-written, helpful, and needed word!"

— Jeff and Rachel G.,
missionaries in Southeast Asia

ALSO BY THE AUTHOR

*Bringing It Home: A Post-Trip Devotional Guide
for International and Domestic Short-Term Mission Teams*

Walking with Paul: A Journey through the Lessons of Ephesians

Getting Along

without

Going Along

Biblical Sexual Ethics In An Age
Of Controversy And Conflict

Jim Mersereau
1 Peter 3:15-16

JIM MERSEREAU

Foresight
Digital Media & Publishing Group

Text copyright © 2018 by Jim Mersereau

Getting Along Without Going Along

Jim Mersereau

Unless otherwise noted all Scripture quotations are from the Holman
Christian Standard Bible, Copyright 1999, 2000, 2002, 2003 by
Holman Bible Publishers. Used by permission. Holman Christian
Standard Bible, Holman CSB, and HCSB are federally registered
trademarks of Holman Bible Publishers. Printed in the United States
of America.

Printed in the United States of America

ISBN 978-1-944265-02-1

All rights reserved. This book is protected by the copyright laws of the
United States of America. This book may not be copied or reprinted
for commercial gain or profit. The use of short quotations or occasional
page copying for personal or group study is permitted and encouraged.
Permission will be granted upon request. No part of this book may be
reproduced without written permission, except for brief quotations in
books and critical reviews.

Foresight Book Publishing
2435 Broad Street
Chattanooga, TN 37408
Visit ForesightPublishingNow.com

Read more from the author at

www.JimMersereauBooks.com

For my church family at Oak Hill Baptist Church

There are two underlying Biblical principles upon which this book is structured. The first is that God's Word is truth. It is the only truth that matters. As Christians we must have and maintain a Biblical worldview in that everything we hear, observe, and experience in the world must be compared to what God tells us in the Bible. The legitimacy of any claim to truth made by the world must be compared to and measured against truth as God reveals it in His Word. As Christians we therefore must know what the Bible says (and what it does not say), and then we must have the boldness and courage to stand for what we know to be true and right.

The second underlying principle, which is directly related to the first, is that as we take our stand for Biblical truth we must do so in the way Peter instructed in 1 Peter 3:15-16, "Always be ready to give a defense to anyone who asks you for a reason for the hope that is in you. However, do this with gentleness and respect …"

Those two Biblical principles are beautifully evident in the life of our church. You are diligent students of the Bible; you are bold and courageous in your witness for Christ and in your proclamation of Biblical truth; but at the same time you are kind and gracious, loving and caring. You know what you believe; you know why you believe it; and you love like Christ loves.

It is my joy and privilege to serve as your pastor.

Contents

Part I
What The Bible Says (And Why It Matters)

Part II
Answers To Difficult Questions

Part III
The Way Forward

Author's Preface

There's an old truism in the world of literature that tells us, "Writers are readers." It's true. To be a writer you must first be a reader. More specifically, you must read (a lot) in the subject you wish to one day write about. That being the case when the writing finally does occur it will necessarily be born of, and rely upon, the many volumes on the subject that were read by the writer before the first word was ever written.

Such is the case with the book you now hold in your hands. I am deeply indebted to numerous writers and speakers on the subject of Biblical sexual ethics and on the various associated cultural issues. Much of what I have written here has been learned from others who have researched, written, and published before me.

Where appropriate, I have cited my sources. However, even in those cases where a citation is not required because I was not directly quoting any one else's work, I still wish to acknowledge my debt to those men and women God has used to inform my thinking and to give me insight on this difficult and emotionally-charged subject. It is my prayer that He will now be able to use my work here to help and inform others, and that we will all be better equipped to boldly, but lovingly take our stand on the truth of God's Word.

Introduction

In 1 Peter 3:15-16 we're told, "Always be ready to give a defense to anyone who asks you for a reason for the hope that is in you. However, do this with gentleness and respect, keeping your conscience clear ..."

Peter's point is that we must speak boldly and confidently about matters of faith. We must know what we believe and why we believe it, and we must be prepared to offer well-reasoned and intelligent explanations about important matters of faith and practice. But we are to do so with gentleness, love, and respect.

And there's the problem. We live in an increasingly polarized society filled with people who passionately disagree on important cultural issues. The rhetoric with which the opposing positions are advocated and defended is often hot and caustic. How can we as Christians be faithful to Peter's directive to faithfully contend for Biblical truth, but do so in a reasoned and respectful manner? How do we avoid getting caught-up in the pulpit-pounding, finger-pointing, overheated and often exaggerated rhetoric flying in both directions?

Not long ago I attended a conference sponsored by the Ethics and Religious Liberty Commission of the Southern Baptist Convention. The theme of the conference was "The Gospel, Homosexuality, and the Future of Marriage." There were more than two thousand church leaders in attendance from forty-eight states and five countries.

As you might expect, the subject that dominated a large part of the conversation was the issue of what is commonly referred to as "The Gay and Lesbian Agenda." There was much discussion about the changing cultural landscape in our society with respect to sexual ethics, the impact those changes are having on our society in general, and on religious liberty in particular.

However, homosexual-related issues were not the only topic discussed. Other areas of sexual ethics were addressed as well including the state of marriage in our nation; no-fault divorce; the increasing number of unmarried, cohabitating, heterosexual couples; polygamy; and much more. It was a well-rounded and thorough look at the entire scope of sexual ethics in America today.

But what impressed me most about the conference was the tone set by the leaders and attendees. There were no fire-breathing, pulpit-pounding, hell-fire and brimstone sermons. There were no angry denunciations and finger-pointing accusations, and there were no hysterical chicken-little types running around crying about the sky falling. Instead the atmosphere was calm, respectful, and even upbeat. The conversation was kind, reasoned, and intellectual. That was especially significant considering that people on all sides of the issue had been invited to attend and participate. So there were conservatives and liberals, Republicans and Democrats, straights and gays. The Gay and Lesbian community had been invited to send representatives to participate, and they did.

Everyone from all camps and from all sides treated each other with respect and kindness. As a result, it was a pleasant and productive conference.

Offering a Biblical response, kindly and respectfully, is what Peter was referring to in 1 Peter 3:15-16. We as followers of Jesus must know what we believe and why we believe it. We must be willing – even eager – to speak-up for Biblical values. But we are to do so in a reasoned and respectful way.

This is the way of Jesus. In the Gospels the only time we see Jesus angry or using strong and even harsh language was when He was dealing with religious hypocrites. With all others His speech and His manner were kind and compassionate—often bold and direct, but kind and compassionate. This is the tone we also must strive for as we interact with others in our society about divisive and potentially emotional, hot-button social issues. The subject of sexual ethics is one of those issues and it is the purpose of this book.

I present the material in the book in a series of short essays, complete with scriptural references and points of practical application. The idea is for the reader to spend time prayerfully thinking through these emotional and divisive issues, allowing the Spirit to speak to your heart at a deeper level.

Each essay addresses a key issue regarding sexual ethics. My goal has been to lead us progressively through the issues, beginning with what the Bible actually says about sexual ethics in general, and about homosexuality in particular. I will attempt to present well-researched and concise discussions about some of the most difficult and confusing aspects of sexual ethics which Christians find themselves confronted with.

Sadly, all too often, Christians are unable to provide reasonable answers for the difficult questions they face. Therefore they lapse into tired clichés and dogma, or worse, they take the path of least resistance and simply choose to drift along with the cultural tide. It is my prayer that these essays will help to correct some of that.

Since much of what is presented here will be unpopular with those who hold opposing views (and therefore subject to argument, debate, and critical analysis), I have paid careful attention to Biblical accuracy. Frequently I also rely on scientific and social science research. In those cases I have given proper attribution and provided footnotes where appropriate. After all, if we're going to stake-out a position on these sensitive issues we should be confident that we are correct. Therefore truth and accuracy are essential.

Also, periodically I will continue to circle back to the subject of attitude. I do this because even the best facts and figures, the most impressive statistics and quotes, the most carefully constructed arguments, achieve nothing if they're delivered in an angry or hurtful way. Our discourse must be characterized by kindness, respect, and love.

It is my prayer that these essays about difficult and emotionally-charged issues will not only inform the reader and provide you with facts rather than just opinions, but that they will also lead all of us to a kinder, gentler, and more Christian way of interacting with those with whom we disagree. May God bless you as you study, think, and pray your way through these essays.

Jim Mersereau
Crossville, TN
April 2018

I
What the Bible Says (And Why It Matters)

Sexual Ethics Matter

"Run from sexual immorality! Every sin a person can commit is outside the body. On the contrary, the person who is sexually immoral sins against his own body. Don't you know that your body is a sanctuary of the Holy Spirit who is in you, whom you have from God? You are not your own, for you were bought at a price. Therefore glorify God in your body."

1 Corinthians 6:18-20

According to the dictionary an "ethic" is "*A system of moral principles or values.*" Therefore a "sexual ethic" is a system of moral principles or values which govern our sexuality. Such a system of principles and values will determine how we think and act when it comes to sexual issues.

We find in the Bible the sexual ethic (the system of moral principles and values pertaining to sexual conduct) which was established by God. This sexual ethic started in the creation, it was further taught in the Old Testament, and it was reaffirmed in the New Testament by Jesus, as well as by Paul and some of the other New Testament writers. It is a sexual ethic which applies to all people in all places for all time. In other words, it applies to everyone, always.

However, over the last fifty years much of the world has been caught-up in a revolution (and a resulting evolution), with respect to sexual ethics. Biblical principles regarding appropriate sexuality have been turned upside down. Worse, in recent times the revolution has begun to snowball and changes to time-honored standards are occurring at an ever-increasing rate. As evidenced in television sitcoms, commercials, and music lyrics, gay marriage, gender identity, cohabitation, a hook-up culture are all being openly promoted as being good and normal.

How are Christians to respond and act in the midst of this? How do we, who are determined to remain faithful to the Biblical sexual ethic, stand strong in the face of ever-increasing cultural pressure and even possible legal action? And not only is the question how should we respond, but what should our attitude and demeanor be when we do?

In the essays which follow we will devotionally explore this very sensitive and divisive issue. We will consider exactly what the Bible does (and does not) say on this issue of sexual ethics. We will discuss the proper attitude with which we are to engage those with whom we disagree, and we will consider strategies for the people of God to navigate this difficult cultural landscape.

But the starting place for us is to recognize that God, the Creator, has in the Bible articulated the sexual ethic which He has established for the entire human race. This is not a cultural issue. It's an issue of Divine will intended for all people in all places at all times. We will begin by examining what the Bible actually says, and does not say. But before we do, let's pause for another word about attitude:

How We Say Things Matters

"A gentle answer turns away anger, but a harsh word stirs up wrath."

Proverbs 15:1

In the introduction to this book, I told you of how impressed I was with the civil tone established and maintained at the conference about sexual ethics in America that I attended. Because the tone was kind and respectful, there was much constructive dialogue. Leaders of the Gay and Lesbian community participated in side meetings with leaders from the Southern Baptist Convention. In comfortable chairs, sipping coffee and munching donuts, they discussed their differences. Reporters from liberal, gay-aligned publications sat side-by-side in the press pool with their peers from strongly conservative media outlets.

The interesting note in all of this is that I'm not aware of anyone on either side having compromised their strongly held beliefs. As far as I could tell, everyone walked away believing pretty much as they did when they walked into those meetings. The important point is not so much that anyone changed their point of view but that sincere people with vastly different perspectives on emotionally charged issues were able to discuss their differences without demonizing each other.

This is significant. There has been far too much overheated and super-charged rhetoric coming from all sides. On the far right, people like those from Westboro Baptist Church in Topeka, KS protest at military funerals holding signs that read "God hates fags" and "Thank God for dead soldiers." On the extreme left, there have been numerous cases of militant Gay and Lesbian activists disrupting church services and vandalizing church property. None of that helps. No cause is advanced by hateful words and destructive actions.

As we go forward now in this series of essays on the subject of sexual ethics, we will consider some of the most emotionally charged cultural issues of our day. But we must do so in a calm and respectful manner, ever-conscious of the fact that all people are deeply loved by God the Father. They are people for whom Jesus died, and it grieves the heart of God if a person ends up lost for eternity.

We are now ready to consider the original sexual ethic established by God the Father at the time of creation, and which was affirmed by Jesus in the Gospels.

God's Standard

"Haven't you read', He replied, 'that He who created them in the beginning made them male and female,' and He also said: 'For this reason a man will leave his father and mother and be joined to his wife, and the two will become one flesh? So they are no longer two, but one flesh. Therefore, what God has joined together, man must not separate.'

Matthew 19:4-6

In the pre-sin world of Eden (recorded in Genesis chapter two), God established His divinely ordained sexual ethic for the human race. He created them male and female. He then instructed that the man and woman should come together as one flesh, and thereby procreate. In the beginning, this was the standard and there was no other. Every other expression of human sexuality outside of the male/female relationship of husband and wife came about after the fall and as a result of sin. And, notably, every other sexual expression which humans have experimented with since then is described by the Bible as being sinful.

In Matthew 19:4-6, in the middle of a discourse to the Pharisees which pertained largely to the issue of divorce, Jesus reaffirmed the Biblical standard for sexual ethics as being between a man and a woman within the bonds of holy matrimony. Nowhere in this passage or in any other do the words of Jesus, or the words of any Biblical writer anywhere in the Bible, allow for any other expression of human sexuality. God could have provided us with examples of other forms of sexual expression which are approved by Him, but He didn't.

This is instructive for us. The Bible provides a complete theology of human sexuality, often in uncomfortable detail. It addresses the full range of possibilities including heterosexual relationship between a husband and wife; sex outside of the bond of marriage; adultery; group sex; incest; bestiality; homosexuality; masturbation; and more. In all cases the teaching is based upon and derived from the core sexual ethic established by God in the beginning. And in all cases any deviation from that core ethic is labeled as sin.

We cannot understand or attempt to apply the teachings of Moses, Jesus, Paul, or any of the Biblical writers on this issue of sexual ethics, without relating it back to Genesis chapter two. The beginning chapters of Genesis are the source from which all the rest of Scripture flows. It is the standard upon which Moses, Jesus, and Paul based their teachings on the subject. The only sexual pairing portrayed in the Bible as being from and approved by God, is that of a man and a woman within the bonds of marriage. Every other expression of human sexuality is labeled as being sinful and outside of the will of God.

Since most of the heated debate in our society today revolves around the issue of homosexuality, that is the issue we will examine first. Not only will we look at what the Bible actually says, but we will also attempt to address some of the most confusing and divisive questions facing Christians today. In the next essay we will consider three Old Testament passages which address this issue.

Instruction from the Old Testament

"You are not to sleep with a man as with a woman; it is detestable."

Leviticus 18:22

A s we proceed in these next essays, giving careful thought to what the Bible teaches regarding same-sex sexual activity, it is imperative that we do so accurately without injecting emotion or personal bias into it. We must simply allow the Bible to speak for itself. We have to be careful we do not try to make it say more than it actually does, and also not less.

Although there are numerous passages all throughout both the Old and New Testaments which teach about sexual ethics, there are only six which speak directly to the issue of homosexuality. There are three in the Old Testament and three in the New Testament. In the Old Testament, they are Genesis chapter 19 (the story of Sodom and Gomorrah); Leviticus 18:22; and Leviticus 20:13.

In recent decades, some revisionist writers have attempted to assign new meaning to those three Old Testament passages, claiming that they do not really teach against monogamous, committed, same-sex relationships. Most notable among those is the book *God and the Gay Christian* by Matthew Vines[1] . I will address Vine's work in a future essay. For now it is enough to say that the new enlightened meaning these modern-day

---

1 Matthew Vines, *God and the Gay Christian* (New York) Convergent Books, 2014

revisionists attempt to assign to these Old Testament passages is in direct contradiction to the universal understanding of these texts by Jewish scholars for almost 3500 years, and by Christian scholars for almost 2000 years.

The sin of Sodom has been universally understood for thousands of years to have been homosexual activity. The same is true of Leviticus 18:22 and 20:13. Also, no distinction was made between a spontaneous homosexual hook-up, and sex within a long-term committed, same-sex relationship. The clear intent of these passages was to express God's disapproval of same-sex sexual activity in any context.

It was necessary for Moses to write of such things, not because same-sex activity was prevalent among the Jews (for the most part it was not), but because it was practiced in the surrounding cultures that the Jews were in close contact with.

In the Genesis account, God established the standard for sexual relations for the human race as being between one man and one woman in marriage. In the story of Sodom we see a great deviation from that God-ordained ethic and we read of God's judgment upon it. Leviticus 18:22 and 20:13 could not possibly be clearer - sexual relations between two people of the same sex are contrary to the expressed will of God.

"You are not to sleep with a man as with a woman ..." 18:22, "If a man sleeps with a man as with a woman, they have both committed a detestable thing ..." 20:13

So God's thoughts about homosexual activity in the Old Testament are clear and indisputable. No serious Old Testament scholar (from ages past or currently), has attempted to impute any meaning to the words other than what the passages clearly state. Next we will consider the three passages from the New Testament which speak directly to the issue of same-sex sexual activity.

Instruction from the New Testament

"This is why God delivered them over to degrading passions. For even their females exchanged natural sexual relations for unnatural ones. The males in the same way also left natural relations with females and were inflamed in their lust for one another. Males committed shameless acts with males and received in their own persons the appropriate penalty of their error."

Romans 1:26-27

It has been rightly said that Romans 1:26-27 is the most significant Bible passage pertaining to the practice of homosexuality. There are two other passages in the New Testament which also speak directly to this issue, 1 Corinthians 6:9 and 1 Timothy 1:10, but Romans 1:26-27 is without question the most important. In this passage Paul reaffirmed that which was so clearly taught in the Old Testament, that God forbids homosexual practice in all circumstances.

However just as with the Old Testament passages regarding homosexuality, there have been attempts made in recent years to redefine what the New Testament passages mean. Matthew Vines and others have attempted to make the case that the three New Testament passages which speak about homosexuality (and this passage in Romans in particular), do not really condemn homosexual acts committed within the structure of a long-term monogamous homosexual relationship.

But the Scripture can only mean what it was intended to mean by those who wrote it. Every study of New Testament Greek conducted by serious and well-trained scholars over the last 2000 years has concluded that this passage forbids sexual relations between individuals of the same sex, regardless of the nature of the relationship. That has been the universal consensus right up until modern times. And even today, it is only those on the extreme fringes of Christian thought, those with a predetermined gay-friendly bias, who are now promoting this new understanding of the text. But what the Bible actually teaches on this subject and what it means (historically and still today) is not in any serious doubt. God was clear. He forbids homosexual activity in all its forms and under all circumstances. Both the Old Testament and the New Testament are perfectly clear on the matter.

However, now that we have seen what the Bible says about homosexual activity, there are still a number of serious and sensitive questions we need to address. Why is it that Jesus never spoke directly about the issue of homosexuality? What about sexual orientation and the possibility that people are born gay? What about "gay rights" in the realm of civil law? But before we address those sensitive and controversial questions, we're going to circle back to where we began this discussion and spend a little more time ensuring we're keeping this all in its proper perspective. It's time for another attitude check.

We Are All
Guilty of Sinning

"Why do you look at the speck in your brother's eye but don't notice the log in your own eye? Or how can you say to your brother, 'Let me take the speck out of your eye,' and look, there's a log in your eye? Hypocrite! First take the log out of your eye, and then you will see clearly to take the speck out of your brother's eye."

Matthew 7:3-5

The Bible is clear in its teaching about homosexual behavior - God prohibits it. However, although we often treat homosexuality as if it's in some special category of sin, God does not. Go back and look at the passages we've identified which specifically mention homosexual behavior and you will discover that the Bible refers to homosexuality right along with a host of other sins. In Leviticus Moses lists it right along with a wide variety of other types of sexual sin. Paul lists it along with idolatry, adultery, greed, murder, envy, stealing, drunkenness, disrespecting parents, profanity and more.

I'm not minimizing the seriousness of homosexuality. My goal remains to simply address it Biblically, and that means fairly and accurately. We must be careful to approach the issue exactly the way God does, in the same context He does. Remember, although homosexuality might not be your sin, yours is listed right along with it.

If there was a meeting of the "Sinners Club" you and I would both be charter members. There would be a seat reserved for you right between the greedy businessman and the homosexual. Seated in front of you would be a lesbian couple and next to them would be the unrepentant glutton. You and I would fit right in and we would discover that there is no distinction made between one sin and another. We are all sinners in need of grace and transformation. Homosexuality is not its own special kind of sin, it's just sin.

The reason the sin of homosexuality gets so much attention from Christians today is because it's one of the only sins which has a highly organized, well-funded, very motivated advocacy group promoting it as a good thing and lobbying for its acceptance. The only other sin I can think of which also falls into this category is abortion (the sin of murder). Because these two sins are so clearly identified in the Bible as being sin, and because their advocacy groups are working so hard to force our society to recognize and accept them as right and good, we as Christians have to be equally motivated to stand for and promote the Biblical truth about them. However, that does not change the fact that you and I are also guilty of our own sins. Jesus illustrated this beautifully in the passage from Matthew 7:3-5 which I cited above, and which comes from the Sermon on the Mount. Yes we do have to advocate for Biblical sexual ethics. But we must do so with a great deal of humility as we remember the truth that we too are sinners saved by grace.

Now it's time to take a closer look at Matthew Vine's book, *God and the Gay Christian*. Then we will move-on to consider some of the difficult questions Christians must be prepared to answer with respect to homosexuality and the impact it is having on our culture today.

Don't Twist Scripture

*"For the time will come when men will not put up with sound doctrine.
Instead, to suit their own desires, they will gather around them a great number
of teachers to say what their itching ears want to hear."*

2 Timothy 4:3 (NIV)

At the time he wrote his book, *God and the Gay Christian,* Matthew Vines was a twenty-four year old professing Christian from Kansas. He was raised in a Christian home and attended a conservative Presbyterian church. Matthew is also openly gay.

After graduating from high school he went off to college at Harvard University. Upon arriving there he was astounded to discover the openness and encouragement he found for the gay lifestyle. After two years at Harvard, Matthew dropped out of college so he could go to work as an advocate for gay Christians.

In 2012 he delivered a speech in a liberal church, attempting to make the case that with respect to homosexuality, the Bible has been misunderstood and misapplied for thousands of years. Matthew attempted to show that the passages which seem to teach against homosexual conduct, actually only apply to lust-driven, short-term hook-ups, not to long-term, committed, homosexual relationships. In order to achieve his purpose, Vines had to engage in a substantial amount of Scripture-twisting and deception but in the end, he was able to construct an argument which on the surface was somewhat convincing to those who were eager to accept it.

The speech was videotaped and posted to YouTube. It went viral and to-date has been viewed over 700,000 times. In early 2014 the speech was published as a book entitled "God and the Gay Christian" and quickly became a best seller.

Matthew admits that he is not a Bible scholar, he has no training in the Biblical languages, and he does not even have a Bible College education. Additionally, the "Bible scholars" whose work he did draw from, mostly all come with a gay-friendly bias and their work is largely dismissed in most of the Christian world.

I bring this to your attention simply because Matthew's video and book have become a sensation in the gay community and are being offered-up as "proof" that God is not opposed to committed, long-term, same-sex relationships.

Dr. Luke Timothy Johnson is a gay New Testament scholar who does have extensive training in the original Biblical languages. He is an advocate for same-sex relationships, but at the same time he is refreshingly honest about what the Bible really does and does not say about it. He writes:

"The task demands intellectual honesty. I have little patience with efforts to make Scripture say something other than what it says … we know what the text says. (However), I think it important to state clearly that we do, in fact, reject the straightforward commands of Scripture, and appeal instead to another authority when we declare that same-sex unions can be holy and good. And what exactly is that authority? We appeal explicitly to the weight of our own experience and the experience thousands of others have witnessed to, which tells us that to claim our own sexual orientation is in fact to accept the way in which God has created us." [2]

What Johnson is saying there is that he knows full well what the Bible says about homosexuality and he doesn't care. He relies instead on how he feels. He then fulfills his desires, and claims God's blessing upon it. That attitude is sad, even tragic, but at least it's honest. Matthew Vines should learn from Luke Johnson. The book *God and the Gay Christian* does not honestly, accurately, or effectively make the case that Vines and his fans claim it does.

---

2 Luke Timothy Johnson and Eve Tushnet, "Homosexuality and the Church: Two Views," *Commonweal* (*June 15, 2007*)

Principles That Apply, And Those That Do Not

"Don't assume that I came to destroy the Law or the Prophets. I did not come to destroy but to fulfill."

Matthew 5:17

As was illustrated in the previous essay, increasingly today, in an effort to normalize homosexual behavior, the authority and accuracy of historical interpretations of the Bible are being challenged. Many of the attacks are sophisticated and on the surface appear somewhat convincing. That, combined with the ever-increasing pressure society is placing upon the Christian community to be tolerant, is leaving many Christians confused and searching for answers. Therefore it's essential that we know what the Bible really does say about the issue, and we must be prepared to respond with accurate and carefully thought-out answers.

One objection that is commonly put forward is that the Old Testament prohibitions regarding homosexual behavior no longer apply in New Testament times. And if we're going to insist that they do, then we are obligated to obey all the other Old Testament prohibitions as well - such as the dietary laws in Leviticus.

So how do we distinguish which Old Testament laws and principles carry over into New Testament times and which do not? The full answer would be somewhat lengthy and complicated, but in general if an Old Testament law or principle was restated or reaffirmed in the New Testament, then it applies to us today; and if it wasn't, then it doesn't. The dietary laws and the prohibition against homosexuality are two contrasting issues that make the case nicely.

In the New Testament, we find that Jesus in Matthew 15:11; Luke in Acts 10:9-15; and Paul in Romans 14:2-3 and again in 1 Corinthians 10:23-31, both made it clear that the Old Testament dietary restrictions no longer applied. But in Romans 1: 26-27, 1 Corinthians 6:9, and 1 Timothy 1:10, Paul affirmed and reinforced the Old Testament prohibition against same-sex relationships. Therefore the dietary laws no longer apply but the prohibitions against homosexual behavior do.

Obviously this point only matters if a person cares what the Bible does or does not say. Not everyone does care. But I'm writing these essays primarily for a Christian audience who does care. The primary purpose here is not to win an argument but instead to provide Christians with good answers to difficult questions. So now we are prepared to answer the charge that Old Testament prohibitions against homosexual behavior don't apply in New Testament times. They do, and now we know why they do.

In the next essay we will give a little more thought to the accuracy and reliability of the historical interpretations of these Bible passages. Then we will move on to the issues of sexual orientation, the apparent silence of Jesus on the subject of homosexuality, issues of civil obedience and disobedience, and much more.

In The Words Of Their Own Scholars

"As some of your own poets have said, 'We are also his offspring."

Acts 17:28 (HCSB)

Before we leave the very important subject of the accuracy and reliability of the historic understanding of what the Bible says and means with respect to homosexuality, I want to share with you a couple of quotes from gay Bible scholars.

In Acts 17:28, when Paul was in Athens attempting to make his case for the truth of the Gospel to Greek intellectuals, he used the words of some of their own scholars to help make his case. I'm doing the same here in this essay.

Dr. Lewis Crompton is a homosexual professor who knows his Bible. He is openly gay and he is a strong advocate for gay causes, but he is also disturbed by the intellectual dishonesty of those who attempt to make the Bible say and mean things it clearly does not say and mean. Perhaps the key passage of Scripture that advocates of the Gay and Lesbian agenda attempt to explain away or distort is Romans 1:26-27:

"This is why God delivered them over to degrading passions. For even their females exchanged natural sexual intercourse for what is unnatural. The males in the same way also left natural sexual intercourse with females and were inflamed in their lust for one another. Males committed shameless

acts with males and received in their own persons the appropriate penalty for their perversion."

With respect to the revisionist attempts to distort Paul's words, Dr. Crompton writes:

"According to this interpretation, Paul's words were not directed at 'bona fide' homosexuals in committed relationships. But such a reading, however well-intentioned, seems strained and unhistorical. Nowhere does Paul or any other Jewish writer of this period imply the least acceptance of same-sex relations under any circumstances." [3]

Dr. Luke Johnson, also a homosexual and a professor of the New Testament, agrees that the New Testament clearly teaches against homosexual relations in all respects, he simply chooses to dismiss what the Bible says:

"We are fully aware of the weight of scriptural evidence pointing away from our position, yet we place our trust in the power of the living God to reveal as powerfully through personal experience and testimony as through written texts." [4]

Johnson further writes that he believes the specific commands of Scripture on this issue are "fallible, conflicting, and often culturally conditioned." Both Crompton and Johnson agree that the Bible says what it says and the meaning is clear. They simply choose to dismiss God's clear teaching on the issue. Instead they allow personal experience and desire to trump Biblical teaching.

Johnson and Crompton are wrong to dismiss the clear teaching of Scripture, but at least they're being honest. If you have to be dishonest to make your case then there must be something fundamentally wrong with the case you are trying to make.

In the next essay we will consider the issue of why Jesus did not specifically mention homosexual behavior in His teachings.

---

3 Lewis Crompton, *Homosexuality and Civilization*, p114 (Boston) Harvard University Press, 2006

4 Johnson, *Commonweal* (June 15, 2007)

II
Answers to
Difficult Questions

The Apparent
Silence of Jesus

"... He who created them in the beginning made them male and female, ... For this reason a man will leave his father and mother and be joined to his wife, and the two will become one flesh."

Matthew 19:5

First, as has already been noted in an earlier essay, in this passage in Matthew chapter nineteen, Jesus restated and reaffirmed the pre-fall sexual ethic established by God in the Garden of Eden. By doing so He implicitly ruled out every other sexual activity that falls outside of the God-ordained pairing of a man and a woman in marriage, including homosexuality.

Second, Jesus didn't mention homosexual behavior specifically because He didn't need to. His ministry while on earth was carried out almost exclusively to the Jews who were geographically located in Biblical Palestine. Homosexual behavior wasn't much of an issue in that culture. Such practices were rare among the Jews and therefore it wasn't necessary for Jesus to teach that lesson to those people.

However in the Old Testament, when the Jews were in close proximity to cultures where homosexual behavior was prevalent, the issue of homosexuality was addressed by Moses. Likewise later in the New Testament, when the Christian faith began spreading outside of Jerusalem and beyond Palestine, the people of God once again found themselves in close proximity to cultures where homosexual behavior was common. So God then had the

Apostle Paul restate and reaffirm the Old Testament prohibitions against it.

The words of Jesus are without question the most important words in the Bible, but they are not the only words in the Bible. God gave us the entire Bible for a reason and all of it is divinely inspired. Jesus Himself did not speak every word that needed to be spoken, and He did not teach every lesson that needed to be taught for all people in all places for all time - but the Bible in its entirety does. When the people of God needed to be told that God forbids sexual relations between people of the same gender, He had Moses do so in the Old Testament and He had Paul take care of it in the New Testament. Therefore it wasn't necessary for Jesus to speak and teach about this issue.

In the next essay we will begin a discussion about sexual orientation. Are people born gay?

Would God Create Someone Gay?

"No one undergoing a trial should say, "I am being tempted by God." For God is not tempted by evil, and He Himself doesn't tempt anyone."

James 1:13

As we consider the issue of sexual orientation and same-sex attraction we must do so with kindness and compassion, but also honestly and accurately. Same-sex attraction is very real and it runs deep. Many people who have a same-sex attraction report having had those attractions from an early age. Likewise, those who demonstrate characteristics and behaviors normally attributed to the opposite gender have usually demonstrated those traits beginning early in life.

Therefore the question is an important one, "Are people born gay?" As we consider the possible answers to that question we must be careful to be Biblically and scientifically honest and accurate. Let's not try to make the Bible or science say more or less than they really do. In this essay we will consider what the Bible does and does not say about this issue. In the next essay we will see what science has to say.

The fact is that there is no passage in either the Old or New Testament which would lead us to conclude that God designs people with a same-sex attraction. As has already been shown, the pre-sin sexual ethic established by God was of a man and a woman expressing human sexuality within the covenant of marriage. That sexual ethic was reaffirmed in the New

Testament by Jesus, Paul, and Peter. Additionally, the six passages we have looked at regarding homosexuality (Genesis 19, Leviticus 18:22 and 20:13, Romans 1:26-27, 1 Corinthians 6:9 and 1 Timothy 1:10) all clearly prohibit same-sex sexual relations.

That being the case, would God then actually design certain individuals to desire to engage in the very behavior He Himself has expressly forbidden? Not only would it make no sense for Him to do that, but it would be cruel to design such a desire into a person but then forbid them to act on it. There is nothing we know about God from the Bible which would cause us to conclude He would do something like that.

Same-sex attraction is undeniably real, but the fact is that there simply is no Biblical basis for concluding that God designs and creates individuals to be sexually attracted to members of the same gender. If He did, then the statement James made in James 1:13 would not be true. God would in fact be creating real temptation for certain individuals.

And yet observing human behavior, even from an early age, seems to suggest otherwise. It can seem as if same-sex attraction must be something that sometimes develops early in an individual's life and must therefore be of a Godly design. There is no easy answer to that difficult issue. But even though the answer is difficult, one cannot reasonably conclude that God creates people gay. The Bible simply does not support such a conclusion.

Perhaps one day we will be able to explain why people sometimes exhibit those traits, even early in life. What we cannot do though, is attribute homosexual desires to God's creative design. The Bible simply does not support such a conclusion.

Today there are loud voices claiming that science *proves* people are born gay. But does it really? Is that an accurate and verifiable claim about what science actually proves? In the next essay we will let the scientific community speak for itself on that question.

Does Science Prove God Creates People With A Same-Sex Attraction?

"For it was You who created my inward parts; You knit me together in my mother's womb. I will praise You because I have been remarkably and wonderfully made."

Psalm 139:13-14

Part of the confusion regarding the issue of sexual orientation lies in the definitions of "orientation" and "design". The dictionary says that an orientation is simply, *"A direction; to make familiar with or adjust to a situation."* In other words, you are oriented towards something when you set out in that direction or when you adjust towards a purpose or thing. Whereas design is: *"The purposeful arrangement of parts or details; a reasoned purpose; intent."*

So as you can see, there's a big difference between orientation and design. Orientation is a decision based upon a choice. Design is part of the inherent nature of the person or thing in question. I find myself "oriented" in the direction of many behaviors I would be better off without, some of them stemming from as early in childhood as I can remember. I also find that the more I engage in those behaviors, the more oriented in that direction I seem to become. But that doesn't mean God designed me that way. Those behaviors are not part of my created design.

The American Psychological Association (APA) has studied this issue in great detail. Many scientific studies have been conducted regarding the nature and source of sexual orientation. After compiling and reviewing a formidable body of scientific research the APA came to some interesting conclusions.

First, with respect to what a sexual "orientation" actually is, they defined it as, *"an enduring pattern of emotional, romantic, and/or sexual attractions to men, women, or both sexes."* [5]

But as to where this attraction comes from the APA was honest when they wrote,

"Although much research has examined the possible genetic, hormonal, developmental, social, and cultural influences on sexual orientation, no findings have emerged that permit scientists to conclude that sexual orientation is determined by any particular factor or factors." [6]

The question we're considering here is not if same-sex attraction is real, it is. There is also no question about whether or not it is deeply rooted within a person, it often is. The question is whether or not God designs some individuals that way. When the APA describes sexual orientation they do so by describing patterns of desire, not genetically driven predispositions. The desires may be deep, and they may be part of lifelong patterns of behavior, but it cannot be said they are genetic.

The honesty of the APA on this subject is helpful but we're not yet finished allowing the scientific community to speak for itself. There is one more very compelling study we need to be aware of with respect to genetic design and same-sex attraction. We will take a look at that in the next essay.

---

5 "Answers to Your Questions: For a Better Understanding of Sexual Orientation and Homosexuality," *American Psychological Association,* 2008, http://www.apa.org/helpcenter/sexual-orientation.aspx

6 Ibid.

Do Gay Twins
Provide Evidence Of
Genetic Cause?

"I will praise You because I have been remarkably and wonderfully made."
Psalm 139:14

Whether or not scientific research points to a genetic cause for sexual orientation is one of the most hotly debated topics in the scientific world today. There have been a large number of studies conducted and they have produced a wide range of findings – much of it contradictory.

The truth is that the studies have not been able to provide conclusive proof one way or the other. That's why, simply as a matter of intellectual honesty, the American Psychological Association (APA) felt compelled to write the statement we read in the previous essay. But likewise for the sake of honesty, I must tell you that the APA also said that they believe the overall trend in the research is leaning in favor of a genetic cause, even though science has not yet been able to prove it.

But then, along comes another study like the one I am about to quote from, the results of which make a strong case for there *not* being a genetic link.

In 2010, researchers in Sweden, working for the "Swedish Twin Registry," surmised that if sexual orientation is a matter of genetic design, then in the case of identical twins there should be observable evidence of identical sexual orientation. Their premise was that because identical twins come from the same egg and share the same genes, and if sexual orientation is genetic, then if one of the twins is gay the other should be also.

The study looked at seventy-one sets of identical twins where at least one was living a homosexual lifestyle. What they discovered was that in only 1 out of 10 cases were both twins gay.[7] In 90% of the cases one twin was gay and the other was not. If there was a genetic cause for sexual orientation then the results should have been exactly the opposite.

As far as many in the scientific community are concerned, the jury is still out regarding whether or not people are born gay. However when all personal bias is removed from the conclusions, honest scientists admit that despite the overwhelming number of studies which have been conducted, they have been unable to demonstrate a genetic cause for sexual orientation.

For Bible-believing Christians this comes as no surprise. As we've already observed, the Bible provides us with no reason to believe that God would create someone gay. And despite science's best efforts, scientists have not been able to prove otherwise.

And yet, same-sex attraction is real and it is deep. So what's the answer for a person who struggles with a same-sex attraction? We will consider that next but first, it's time for another attitude check.

---

7 Stanton L. Jones, *Sexual Orientation and Reason: On the Implications of False Beliefs and Homosexuality*, 8.
, http://www.wheaton.edu/CACE/CACE-Print-Resources/~/media/Files/Centers-and-Institutes/CACE/articles/Sexual%20Orientation%20and%30Reason%20%201-9-20122.pdf.

A Quiet Sense
Of Confidence

"Then justice will inhabit the wilderness, and righteousness will dwell in the orchard. The result of righteousness will be peace; the effect of righteousness will be quiet confidence forever."

Isaiah 32:16-17

I love the scene described in Isaiah 32:16-17. The prophet was painting a picture of the Messianic Kingdom. He was explaining that at that time righteousness and noble values will reign, and that will produce in God's people a quiet sense of confidence.

You may remember from the introduction to this book when I explained how impressed I was with the tone that was set at the conference on sexual ethics that I attended. Even though the subject was serious and difficult, the tone was friendly and kind, compassionate and even upbeat. One reason it was that way was because the conference leaders and attendees had a quiet sense of confidence. They had taken the time to prayerfully think through the issues, and they did their homework so that they were thoroughly familiar with both sides of the issues. That then gave them a quiet sense of confidence. Because they were sure of what they believed and why they believed it, they were able to calmly and rationally discuss the issues without getting upset or defensive. We need more of that.

That's why I'm writing this series of essays on sexual ethics. Far too many Christians do not have enough accurate information to enable them to feel confident explaining their beliefs or discussing the difficult issues. That lack of confidence often leads people to feel insecure and defensive.

That then sometimes leads to the use of overheated language. Please don't come across as hard-hearted, mean-spirited, or insensitive. Doing so won't win any arguments. It will only further inflame the situation and it will actually drive people further away rather than drawing them near.

My goal with this series of essays is to provide the reader with enough accurate information so that you will feel confident discussing the issues with those who may disagree with you. The starting place should always be compassion, kindness and love. Then move-on to some basic Biblical truths. Finally, be ready to give good answers to some of the more difficult questions (such as those we have discussed so far and which we will continue to explore as we go forward in this series).

Next we will think some more about the very real struggle of same-sex attraction, and we will consider some ideas about how to deal with it.

Your Desires
Don't Define You

"Dear friends, I urge you as strangers and temporary residents to abstain from fleshly desires that war against you."

1 Peter 2:11

Sam Allberry is the author of the book *Is God Anti-Gay?* He serves as the Associate Pastor of St. Mary's Church in Maidenhead, United Kingdom. Sam is also a celibate gay man. He has experienced same-sex attractions for as long as he can remember, and for many years he acted on those attractions.

Eventually though, Sam came to the point when he had to admit that there simply was no way his lifestyle could be Biblically justified. He realized he had deep desires which he could no longer in good conscience act on. Through prayer, Bible study, and deep thought, he came to some interesting and helpful insights that he shared with the rest of us in his book.

First, Sam finally came to see that although the Bible clearly portrays homosexual desires as being unnatural and contrary to the will of God, they are described that way right along with a whole host of other desires that are also unnatural and contrary to the will of God. That being the case, he decided he needed to exercise discipline and refrain from acting on those homosexual desires, just as all people are to refrain from acting on the desires of greed, or over-indulgence in alcohol, or heterosexual lust, or any of the other sins on the list.

If we keep homosexual activity in its proper Biblical context, and include it right along with all the other sinful acts we are to refrain from, we see that a person's response to it needs to be the same as to any other sinful desire. This is what Peter was writing about in 1 Peter 2:11 (quoted above).

Allberry writes, "*We live in a culture where sexuality is virtually equated with identity: 'You are your sexuality.' We are encouraged to think that to experience homosexual feelings means that you are, at your most fundamental core, a homosexual ... My own perception is that I struggle with greed much more than I do with sexual temptation.*"[8]

Allberry's point is crucial - your desires do not define you. As a Christian it is your identity in Christ that defines you. Desires and behaviors contrary to the expressed will of God are symptoms of living in a fallen and broken world. But in your inner-most being you are defined by your identity in Christ, not by your sexual attractions, or by your overeating, or your preoccupation with material possessions, or with any other desire or behavior. Your desires do not define you.

This subject of our true identity in Christ, and how it relates to same-sex attractions, is just too important to address in a single essay. There is much more we need to consider. Therefore we will continue this discussion in the next essay.

8   Sam Alberry, *Is God Anti-Gay?* (UK) The Good Book Company, 2013, p46

We Do Not Have To Act On Our Desires

"I say then, walk by the Spirit and you will not carry out the desire of the flesh. For the flesh desires what is against the Spirit, and the Spirit desires what is against the flesh."

Galatians 5:16-17

The truth is that we all have strong desires we are repeatedly tempted to act on. Some of those desires run deep and last a lifetime. Homosexual desire can certainly fall into that category.

As we learned in the previous essay from the writing of Pastor Sam Allberry, if you struggle with same-sex attraction that is something *about* you, but it is not you. It does not define who you are. If you are a Christian, then same-sex attraction is not your core identity and it does not have to define, dominate, or drive your life. Just as with any other unbiblical desire we have, the Bible instructs us to control it by living under the guidance and power of the Holy Spirit.

That's often not the answer we want. Submitting our desires to Christ and then learning to control them is seldom easy, but it is always right. Sam Allberry is just one of many sincere Christians who struggle with same-sex attraction but who have made the decision to bring that desire, right along with all other desires, under the control and dominion of the Holy Spirit.

In his book, *Love into Light* [9] pastor Peter Hubbard tells the story of the great Christian writer C.S. Lewis, who lived most of his life as a celibate

---

9   Peter Hubbard, *Love Into Light* (Greenville), Ambassador International, 2013

single man. (He was married for a very brief time later in life, but after a short marriage his wife suddenly and tragically died.) There's no indication that C.S. Lewis had any homosexual tendencies himself, but within his university community of professors and writers in England during the time of World War Two, there were many homosexuals whom Lewis knew and was friends with.

Lewis gave much thought to how a Christian with same-sex attractions could live a life that was Biblically obedient and which brought honor and glory to Christ. He concluded that homosexual desire needed to be handled exactly the same as any other desire of the flesh that was contrary to the expressed will of God. Lewis explained that the physical satisfaction of homosexual desire is sin. But then he drew a parallel between the ongoing struggle to gain control over same-sex desires, with the man born blind in the Gospel of John Chapter Nine. In that scene the disciples wanted to know why God had allowed the man to be born blind. Without going into great detail here, the essence of Jesus' answer was that through the physical disability of blindness, there was an opportunity for God to be glorified.

The point Lewis was making with his illustration was that any unnatural desire, any physical disability, any sickness, or any struggle with sin, can become a vehicle through which that person shines for Jesus in the way in which they deal with it. He said that our struggle with any of those issues must be offered up to God.

Yes, same-sex attraction is real and deep and difficult, but so are many other things we struggle with in this life and in all of it we can honor, glorify, and magnify God in how we deal with it.

How does a person with a strong same-sex attraction accomplish this? In the next essay we will discuss the issue of singleness. Many people (not just those with a same-sex attraction), live single and celibate lives. What does the Bible have to say about this?

Being Single Is Okay

"An unmarried man is concerned about the things of the Lord – how he may please the Lord. But a married man is concerned about the things of the world – how he may please his wife – and his interests are divided."

1 Corinthians 7:32-34

I read an article in the newspaper which reported that the U.S. Census Bureau has discovered that more than half of all the adults in our country today are not married. Some have never married, others have married and divorced, others are widows or widowers, but more than half of the adults in our country are not married.

Being single is often viewed as an unfortunate condition that we need to help the single person correct. This can be especially true in Christian circles but that's not an accurate description of singleness and it's also not Biblical. Certainly there are some singles who are lonely and who long for a partner to go through life with, but many others do not feel that way.

Years ago I was speaking about this with a middle-aged single woman in our church. She was an attractive professional woman who had a rewarding and fulfilling career in public service. She was active in civic organizations, and she was also very involved in the life of our church. Her relationship with the Lord was deep, she had a circle of close friends, and she had hobbies and interests such as music, reading, and sports. In short, she had a good life. The comment she made to me about her singleness (which has stuck with me all these years) was, "Pastor, I live alone but I am not lonely. I love my life. It is rich and full and rewarding and I'm very happy."

A false assumption many of us make is that people have to be married or in a romantic relationship in order to be happy. That argument is frequently made when it comes to the subject of same-sex relationships. It is often said that it would be unfair and perhaps even cruel to suggest that the individual with a same-sex attraction should opt for a single and celibate life rather than a homosexual relationship.

But a single life of celibacy is not cruel or unfair - it is Biblical. In 1 Corinthians 7:32-34 the Apostle Paul recommended the single life for the sake of deeper spirituality and greater service to the Lord. It was the life that he lived, as did Jesus, and so have many others.

Same-sex attraction is undeniably real, but so are many other attractions and desires which the Bible forbids us to act on. It is possible to bring all such desires under the control of the Holy Spirit and to then live a life within Biblical boundaries. In the next essay we will consider the stories of several Christians with same-sex attraction who have chosen, and are very happy with, a single and celibate life.

We Do Not Have To
Be Sexually Active

"You took off your former way of life, the old self that is corrupted by deceitful desires; you are being renewed in the spirit of your minds; you put on the new self, the one created according to God's likeness in righteousness and purity of the truth."

Ephesians 4:22-24

No, everybody is not "doing it". I'm talking about sex. In our sex-saturated society the common belief is that everyone is sexually active. But that's just not true. People engage in sexual activity a lot less frequently than the culture would have us believe. And there are many more people living lives of complete celibacy than most of us realize.

C.S. Lewis lived most of his life single and celibate, and so have more people than I have time or space to list here. Countless others have had romantic and sexual relationships during a season of life, but then spent many more years living a celibate life. It's not the end of the world. It's not even a bad thing. The Bible actually commends it.

Too often the argument is made these days that gay relationships should be accepted and endorsed (regardless of what God has said in the Bible) because it would be unnatural and unreasonable to expect the person with a same-sex attraction to forego sex and romance. But that's a paper-thin argument which simply doesn't stand-up to close scrutiny.

In a previous essay I told you the story of Pastor Sam Allberry. He leads a full and happy life as a single and celibate man who happens to have same-sex attractions. Christopher Yuan is another. He was a radical gay activist who had more homosexual encounters than he could count.

But once he came to faith in Christ he realized that the Word of God made no allowances for a homosexual lifestyle of any sort. He too now lives as a single and celibate man who continues to have same-sex attractions, but who has surrendered them to the control of the Holy Spirit. I encourage you to read his book *Out of a Far Country*[10]. By the way, today Christopher is a professor at Moody Bible Institute.

Rosaria Butterfield has a similar story with a slightly different ending. Rosaria was a liberal college professor and by her own definition she was a "radical lesbian feminist." Rosaria didn't just agree with and support the Gay and Lesbian agenda - she was one of the leaders of it. At one point she met a pastor and his wife who simply wanted to have a discussion with her regarding gay issues. She reluctantly agreed to talk to them and was soon impressed with their kind and respectful manner. Over a long period of time they developed an ongoing friendship and spent many hours discussing their differing perspectives. Eventually Rosaria was captured by the love of Christ and she became a Christian. She then left her lesbian lover and committed to living as a single and celibate disciple of Christ.

To her amazement however, over time she discovered that God was actually changing her desires. She found that her attraction to other females was fading, and then one day she actually met a *man* she was attracted too. Long story short, Rosaria ended up marrying that man, they had children, and today she is a happy pastor's wife. Yes that's right, a "pastor's" wife. Her husband is a pastor and she serves happily and well as a pastor's wife. You can read her story in her book *The Secret Thoughts of an Unlikely Convert*[11].

Same-sex attractions are real, but no person has to be held captive to them. Christ can give us victory over those desires (and over every other desire) that is contrary to the clear teaching of the Word of God.

Next we will tackle another difficult and controversial question: "Is it possible to be Christian and gay?

---

10 Christopher Yuan, Angela Yuan, and Kay Warren, *Out of a Far Country* (Colorado Springs: WaterBrook Press, 2011)

11 Rosaria Champagne Butterfield, *The Secret Thoughts of an Unlikely Convert* (Pittsburgh: Crown and Covenant Publications, 2012)

Can A Person Be Gay and Christian?

"Don't you know that the unrighteous will not inherit God's kingdom? Do not be deceived: No sexually immoral people, idolaters, adulterers, or anyone practicing homosexuality, no thieves, greedy people, or swindlers, will inherit God's kingdom."

1 Corinthians 6:9-10

Can a person be gay and be a Christian? It's a perplexing and difficult question that people on both sides of the cultural divide often get quite passionate about. And there is no easy answer to it.

In 1 Corinthians 6:9-10 Paul tells us that homosexuals will not inherit the kingdom of God. But he also says the same about immoral people in general, and about those who commit heterosexual adultery. He includes in that list those who treat anything as an idol, and those who steal, and those who are greedy, and those who are deceitful, and those who swindle others.

Also, this list was not all-inclusive. Paul intended it to only be representative of sins in general. You can go ahead and assume that even if your personal sins are not on that list, Paul intended for you to understand that he includes them as well. Look at the passage again - the phrase "the unrighteous" covers any sins he happened to leave off his list.

So with that understanding we realize that if homosexuals are excluded from heaven, then we all are. And yet we know that even though we do still sometimes commit sins, if we have placed our faith in Jesus Christ for the forgiveness of our sins then we are saved and we are going to heaven. Therefore we will in fact inherit God's kingdom. So what could Paul mean?

He was writing about unrepentant sin. He was illustrating that people who live in a perpetual pattern of unrepentant sin (be it adultery, greed, homosexuality, idolatry, or any other pattern of unrepentant sin) are probably not really saved.

We know that one of the Holy Spirit's jobs is to convict us of sin. If a person really does have the Holy Spirit of God in their heart then that person should at least be sorry for the sin they have committed and have a genuine desire to do it no more. If a person does not feel sorry and convicted about sinful behavior, we have to wonder where the Spirit is. Evidently He's not in that person's heart or they would feel convicted.

Is it possible to be a practicing homosexual and to be a Christian? Yes, I suppose it is. Just as it's possible to be a greedy businessman and be a Christian; just as it's possible to be an alcoholic and be a Christian; just as it's possible to be a glutton and be a Christian. But if you are a Christian, you should feel convicted of such behavior and if you don't feel convicted, you have to wonder about whether or not you are really a Christian.

Determining whether any person is truly saved is beyond the scope of our spiritual knowledge. All we can do is observe their life to see if their behavior is consistent with that of a person who has the Holy Spirit of God in their heart. If it isn't, we still cannot say for sure if the person is saved or not, only God knows that. But we should assume that they're not saved and then go to work to lead them to faith in Christ.

In the next essay we will address the subject of same-sex marriage.

The Bible Makes No Provision For Same-Sex Marriage

"'Haven't you read,' He replied, 'that He who created them in the beginning made them male and female,' and He also said: 'For this reason a man will leave his father and mother and be joined to his wife, and the two will become on flesh?'"

Matthew 19:4-5

G ay marriage is one of the most contentious and difficult cultural issues facing Christians today. How should a Bible-believing Christian think about and respond to this emotionally-charged, hot-button issue?

First, at this point in our study it should be abundantly clear that the Bible makes no provision for same-sex marriage. As has already been clearly demonstrated, the Biblical standard for all expressions of human sexuality is the pre-sin standard established by God in Genesis chapter two and reaffirmed by Jesus in Matthew chapter nineteen. The standard is one man and one woman committed to each other in a lifelong marriage. This was also affirmed by Paul in Ephesians 5:22-33 and by Peter in 1 Peter 3:1-7.

In an effort to weaken the argument that the Biblical standard is limited to only one man and one woman, some advocates of gay marriage point to the fact that polygamy was practiced by some of the Old Testament patriarchs such as Abraham and Jacob. Therefore since polygamy involves more than just one man and one woman, other combinations must be okay too.

But nowhere in the Bible is polygamy endorsed. And in every case (especially with Jacob), we read that it produced numerous family problems. In the Old Testament polygamy was a practice some of the Jews engaged in for a brief period in their history, but it was never God's original design. Beyond that, there is no evidence of it in the New Testament at all. Also, in Galatians 4:21-31, the Apostle Paul writes in a critical manner regarding the results of Abraham's polygamy.

There can be no question that the Biblical standard for marriage involves one man and one woman in a committed relationship for life. That was God's original design and it is reaffirmed in the New Testament. That means there cannot be a Biblical justification for gay marriage, and that should answer the question for Bible-believing Christians, which then reduces the question to a cultural one rather than a Biblical one.

In a future essay we will think about the cultural dimensions of gay marriage but before that, we need to think a little more about the Biblical case for traditional marriage. This is an important issue which needs a little further exploration because in our day more and more Christians, especially young ones, are coming to the unbiblical conclusion that gay marriage might just be okay.

Same-Sex Marriage Cannot Be Biblically Justified

"For this reason a man will leave his father and mother and be joined to his wife, and the two will become one flesh."

Ephesians 5:31

In Ephesians 5:31 Paul quoted, and therefore reaffirmed, the words of Moses in Genesis 2:24. Those identical words also appear in Matthew 19:5 and Mark 10:7-8. Additionally, Malachi 2:15 and 1 Corinthians 6:16 express the exact same thought using only slightly different words. The same point made six times. Do you think God might have been trying to tell us something?

As was noted in the previous essay, there simply is no verse or passage in the Bible which can in any way be made to imply that a marriage between two people of the same gender is okay with God. It is not. Six passages specifically state the God-ordained, Biblical model of marriage as being between one man and one woman for a lifetime. Six other passages directly forbid same-sex sexual relations of any type under any circumstances.

In the book *God and the Gay Christian? - A response to Matthew Vines*, Professor of Biblical studies at Boyce College Denny Burk contributed an essay which addressed this issue. In his essay, Professor Burk wrote that Biblical marriage must be reflective and symbolic of the gospel (as described by Paul in Ephesians 5:22-31.) The imagery is clearly and intentionally male/female, husband/wife. But there is no way same-sex marriage can be made to fit that model. Burk also notes that:

"Jesus defines the marriage covenant in Matthew 19 as a monogamous heterosexual union." [12]

Since there clearly is no Biblical sanction for a marriage between two people of the same gender, and since the Bible is the foundation and guide for all of Christian thought, belief, and practice, it becomes unthinkable for a Bible-believing Christian to endorse or promote gay marriage. To do so would be to disregard the clear teaching of Scripture.

Therefore, since we now know there is no Biblical justification for same-sex marriage we realize that if there is any rationale for it at all, that rationale would have to be cultural. Are there good cultural reasons to endorse, encourage, promote, and even legalize gay marriage? We will discuss the cultural dimensions of it in the next essay.

---

12 *God and the Gay Christian? A Response to Matthew Vines*, R. Albert Mohler Jr. editor, (Louisville: SBTS Press, 2014), p53

A Brave New World?

"Therefore God delivered them over in the cravings of their hearts to sexual impurity, so that their bodies were degraded among themselves. They exchanged the truth of God for a lie ..."

Romans 1:24-25

Perhaps what's most frustrating about the current cultural trend to normalize same-sex marriage is the dishonest way in which it is being promoted. Advocates for gay marriage portray it as benign, harmless, and even natural. They express bewilderment that any right-minded and reasonable person would object to it.

What is left unsaid is that no society ever, at any point in human history, has even suggested that same-sex pairings are the same as a marriage between a man and a woman. Never mind legalizing such couplings and establishing them as a cultural norm, no society in the history of the human race has ever even considered equating homosexual relationships on par with a marriage between a man and a woman.

This is an important point. What's being promoted in our day as normal, natural, benign, and harmless, is actually something entirely new in the history of the human race. Legalized and normalized marriage between two people of the same sex is a seismic, cultural shift unlike anything that has ever happened before.

The proponents of gay marriage should at least be honest in the way they portray it. This is not a contemporary version of the Hallmark Channel television show "The Walton's." This is not Norman Rockwell for 2018. This is more like "A Brave New World." If people of previous generations could have gazed into a crystal ball and seen our cultural condition today, they would have been shocked and appalled.

There is no question that a marriage between two people of the same sex is contrary to God's design. The Bible could not be clearer on the subject. So why is God allowing this to occur? Romans 1:24-25 explains it well. It is because God made Himself clear on the issue. If society is going to forge ahead anyway with something that is obviously contrary to His expressed will, He will allow it to happen and He will then allow that society to suffer the consequences of its choices.

In the next essay we will consider what some of those consequences could be.

The Outcome
Cannot Be Good

"They are a nation without sense; there is no discernment in them. If only they were wise and would understand this and discern what their end will be!"

Deuteronomy 32:28-29

In some respects it's impossible to accurately forecast what the long-term impact of legalized same-sex marriage will have on our society. However, since it's obviously contrary to the expressed will of God, we have to conclude that the impact will be bad. But how bad and in what ways remains to be seen.

Historically, virtually all societies have recognized the value and importance of the traditional family structure. When a father, mother, and children constitute a stable family unit, it creates a safe and nurturing environment for children to grow; and the more of those family units that exist in a society, the stronger and more stable that society tends to be. That's simply observable and well documented history, and the vast majority of sociological studies conducted on the issue have confirmed it.

Dr. Glenn Stanton, the director of Global Family Formation Studies at Focus on the Family, writes that *"Despite the high divorce rate among heterosexual couples in America, marriage between a man and a woman is still by far the most stable home environment for children."* [13] He notes that in Scandinavia, perhaps the most gay-friendly place in the world, studies

---

13   *Glenn T. Stanton "What we can learn from same sex couples", https://glenntstanton.com/homosexuality.*

have revealed that same-sex male marriages break- up at twice the rate of heterosexual marriages, and same-sex female relationships break-up at twice the rate of male/male pairings. Although everyone can point to some same-sex relationships which have endured, the research is conclusive that overall, same-sex relationships break-up at a rate far higher than heterosexual relationships. Therefore same-sex family structures in general provide an unstable environment in which to raise children.

It will probably be another fifty years before accurate assessments can be conducted to determine what impact the legalization of same-sex marriage ultimately had on our society. But of course by then it will be too late, the impact will have already occurred. Because legalized same-sex marriage is something entirely new in the history of the human race, there simply is no historical precedent we can study which can be used to help us gauge where this is likely to lead or what effect it will have on society.

What we do know is that same-sex marriage is contrary to God's design and therefore the outcome cannot be good. In the next essay we will begin to consider transgender and transsexual issues.

God Created Us
Male and Female

"A woman is not to wear male clothing, and a man is not to put on a woman's garment, for everyone who does these things is detestable to the Lord your God."

Deuteronomy 22:5

Although Deuteronomy 22:5 is an Old Testament prohibition given to the nation of Israel, and although it is included in a long list of other prohibitions which no longer pertain to the people of God in this day, this one does still apply. It still applies today because it is consistent with the Biblical sexual ethic that God created us as male and female, and with the clear Biblical teaching that He intends for us to conduct ourselves within the boundaries of those gender identities.

The editors of the Holman Christian Standard Study Bible are helpful: *"For a woman to wear male clothing and a man a woman's garment (crossdressing or transvestitism) is wrong because, among other things, it violates the principle of separation that God has built into the created order."* [14]

For the sake of clarity some definitions are needed here. The terms "transgender" and "transsexual" are often used interchangeably and mean, "Appearing as or having undergone surgery to become a member of the opposite sex."

An important note here is that a person's decision to present themselves as a member of the opposite sex, either by means of clothing or surgery, is

---

14   HCSB Study Bible, (Nashville: Holman Bible Publishers, 2010) , p 318

based on feelings not biology. The individual has a desire to present themselves as a member of the opposite sex and then takes steps to do so. There is no medical evidence proving such desires and feelings are biologically driven.

There is a very rare biological condition known as "intersex" whereby an individual is born with a mix of both male and female biological characteristics. These could include mixed genitalia, a mix of both male and female chromosomes, or internal reproductive anatomy that doesn't match external features. These conditions are rare. Typically parents and doctors make a sex assignment decision at birth and the individual is then raised with that gender identity. Interestingly though, in the vast majority of those cases, there is no gender confusion experienced and the individual goes through life comfortable with their assigned gender identity. Therefore such cases rarely enter into the transgender / transsexual debate.

Culturally, transgender issues are being lumped right in with the rest of the Gay and Lesbian Agenda. Many municipalities and school districts are considering legislation to allow transgender people to utilize the dressing rooms, locker rooms, and rest rooms for the gender they identify as. Conceivably this could mean that a 14 year old boy (with all the sexual equipment of a 14 year old boy) who is feeling pretty today, and therefore decides to wear a dress to school, would be allowed to use the girl's locker room and the girl's rest room - right alongside your 14 year old daughter. (This stuff is real and it is actually happening in our day).

Transgender issues are similar to same-sex attraction in that the desires are real and they often run deep. As Christians, our response needs to be the same. With respect and kindness, but also with confidence and boldness, we must insist that transgender desires, along with all other unbiblical desires human beings experience, can and should be brought under the control of the Holy Spirit.

We have two more "sexual ethics" issues to consider – cohabitation and casual sex, and then we will conclude our study by considering strategies and actions the Christian community can and must take in response to the sexual ethics revolution taking place in our society today. Take heart – all is not lost!

Casual Sex

*"Why, my son, would you be infatuated with a forbidden woman or embrace
the breast of a stranger?"*

Proverbs 5:20

As a teenager I grew-up during the height of the hippie movement.
That was the "free love" generation. The idea was that love was the
answer to the world's problems and if we would all just be more intentional
and less inhibited about expressing love, the problems of the world would
magically melt away.

Although lip service was paid to the values of kindness and compassion,
the primary expression of "free love" was "free sex." There was a popular
Rock and Roll group by the name of "Crosby, Stills, Nash, and Young" who
had a hit song with the chorus, "If you can't be with the one you love - then
love the one you're with." And so we did.

Eventually the hippies grew-up, got jobs and had kids, and the hippie
movement faded away but the free love movement did not. Instead it
morphed into a culture of casual sex which is still very much alive in our
society today. Among young people it's known as "hooking up." This is the
notion that guys and girls who have an attraction to each other can "hook
up" for a sexual encounter without being encumbered by any commitments
which extend beyond the moment.

There's also another form of casual, sexual relationship which exists
today known as "friends with benefits." These are men and women who

are close friends and who have no romantic feelings for each other, but who come together from time to time to meet each other's sexual needs. Once the encounter is over their friendship continues as before, but still with no romantic feelings and certainly no commitments.

All of the sexual relationships just described are clearly outside the Biblical sexual ethic established by God of one man and one woman in a committed lifelong marriage. They are unbiblical and therefore sinful. Beyond that, casual sex is destructive. The sex act was intended by God to be a holy moment of intimacy shared by a husband and wife. Casual sex cheapens the sex act and undermines the sanctity of traditional marriage. Additionally, casual sex transmits disease. Sexually transmitted disease (STD) is a major health issue today. STDs are widespread and if you engage in enough casual sex, you will eventually contract one. However there is one easy way to avoid contracting a STD - simply marry a person who doesn't have one and then never have sex with anyone else.

As the Church, we must boldly and confidently preach, teach, and promote the Biblical standard of sexual ethics. Then we must practice it ourselves. We must be the champions of traditional Biblical marriage. The culture should be able to look to the church to see examples of healthy married couples, and celibate singles, all of whom honor God in their sexual lives.

In the next essay we will consider the issue of cohabitation, sometimes referred to as common-law marriage.

Cohabitation:
An Acceptable Alternative
to Marriage?

"For you have had five husbands, and the man you have now is not your husband."

John 4:18

Cohabitation simply means "to live together as spouses when not legally married." When a man and woman live together sharing a home and a bed, but without being legally married, they are cohabitating. This is also sometimes referred to as a "common-law marriage."

In John 4:18 Jesus was in a conversation with a Samaritan woman. As the verse indicates, she had been married and divorced numerous times and was at that time living with a man she was not married to. The implication of Jesus' words was that it was wrong for her to be doing so. In the *MacArthur Study Bible* pastor John MacArthur explains:

"She was living conjugally with a man whom Jesus said was not her husband. By such an explicit statement, our Lord rejected the notion that when two people live together it constitutes marriage. Biblically, marriage is always restricted to a public, formal, official, and recognized covenant." [15]

In our sexually liberated society, cohabitation has become increasingly common. Estimates vary widely but it is generally agreed that as many as 30% of young couples will live together for some period of time prior to marrying. There are many reasons for this. Sometimes they believe

---

15   "The MacArthur Study Bible" (Nashville: Word Publishing, 1997), p1584

that living together will help them gauge whether or not a marriage will be successful. Interestingly however, studies show that couples who live together first and then marry, end up divorcing at a higher rate than those who don't cohabitate first.

Sometimes people cohabitate because the woman has children already and she is receiving various forms of public assistance such as food stamps and subsidized housing. The concern is that if she were to marry, some or all of the public assistance would stop. We sometimes find older couples cohabiting for a similar reason. A widow or widower may be receiving survivor's benefits from the retirement plan of a deceased spouse and often there is a provision that if the person remarries, the benefits are reduced or stopped.

There can be many rationalizations for cohabiting, but a Christian cannot escape the fact that the Bible does not allow for it. Even in those cases where there are very real financial considerations, we must make a decision to honor the Lord and then trust Him to take care of us. In Matthew 6:25-33 Jesus made it clear that our Father is fully aware of all our needs and He will provide for us. Our part is to *"seek first the kingdom of God and His righteousness, and all these things will be provided for you."*

In the next essay we will consider the problem of pornography. Then we will conclude our study of sexual ethics by discussing strategies and actions Christians and the Church can take as we continue to live-out our faith amidst the seismic moral shift that is occurring in our society today.

Pornography Is A Sin

"But I tell you, everyone who looks at a woman to lust for her has already committed adultery with her in his heart."

Matthew 5:28

I remember when I was a young boy in the late 50s and early 60s, women's underwear ads were rare and a bit controversial. I have to admit that I did look for them in the Sunday ads in the newspaper (but I always felt a little guilty if I found one).

Today naked women adorn the covers of magazines at the check-out counters in most stores; steamy love scenes are regular fare on television shows during the "family" hour; and sexy models in Victoria's Secret lingerie sell everything from beer to bacon.

Journalist Pamela Paul says that we now live in a "pornified" culture.[16] I think she's right. The glorification of sex has overwhelmed us. It's everywhere. We are over-sexed. You would think that when something becomes so overdone and so pervasive, we would become desensitized to it. Apparently the exact opposite is true. As a nation we seem to be obsessed with sex, and our appetite for evermore explicit sexual images seems to be continually increasing. The stuff that previous generations considered "hardcore," such as Playboy magazine, is considered pretty tame by today's standards. Today the hardcore stuff comes to us over the internet and it is

16 Pamela Paul, *Pornified: How Pornography Is Damaging Our lives, Our Relationships, and Our Families* (New York: Owl Books, 2005)

seriously hardcore. I'm talking about gay-porn, child-porn, group sex, bestiality, and more.

Statistics vary, but they suggest that somewhere around 60% of men view pornography on a regular basis. One study I saw recently said that perhaps 50% of men "in the church" view pornography at least once a month, and in one survey 20% of pastors admitted to it, and women are not exempt. Those same studies tell us that 20-25% of women admit to viewing pornography once or more a month.

Pornography is not innocent. Jesus taught in Matthew 5:28 that imagining yourself in the commission of a sinful act is effectively no different than actually committing the sinful act. As far as He is concerned, if you imagined yourself doing it, then you did do it.

As the people of God, we are exhorted to be holy because God is holy. We are to strive for purity in thought, word, and deed. Paul wrote, *"Finally brothers, whatever is true, whatever is honorable, whatever is pure, whatever is lovely, whatever is commendable – if there is any moral excellence and if there is any praise – dwell on these things." Philippians 4:8*

Pornography pollutes the mind, diminishes purity, and corrupts character. As Christians we must be intentional about safeguarding our mind and heart from the pornographic images and suggestions that have become so much a part of the culture we live in.

Next, as we begin to draw our study to a close, we will consider some actions and strategies we can all take to honor God and to effectively engage our culture in this area of sexual ethics.

III

The Way Forward

A Moral Revolution

"Woe to those who call evil good and good evil, who substitute darkness for light and light for darkness, who substitute bitter for sweet and sweet for bitter."

Isaiah 5:20

In America the cultural norms for acceptable sexual ethics were pretty stable for most of our history. From the days of the Pilgrims right up through the 1950's, the Biblical standard for sexual behavior was overwhelmingly accepted and mostly unquestioned. The sexual revolution of the hippie years initiated the beginnings of a cultural shift, but it has only been in the last twenty-five years that the Biblical standard has been directly challenged on the national level.

Dr. Albert Mohler, the President of Southern Baptist Seminary, helps us to understand what happened. He refers to the work of British philosopher Theo Hobson, who developed a theory regarding how to initiate a moral revolution within a culture[17]. Dr. Hobson taught that in order to bring about a moral revolution in a culture, there are three basic steps or phases which must be deliberately passed through. First, the moral beliefs and behaviors which used to be condemned must now be celebrated. Second, the moral beliefs and behaviors that used to be celebrated must now be condemned. And third, those who refuse to celebrate the new moral standards and behaviors must also be condemned. This is exactly what has

---

17   www.albertmohler.com, "The Briefing : 05-16-16"

happened in our society with respect to sexual ethics.

Dr. Mohler explains that moral revolutions of the kind described by Theo Hobson have occurred at various times in different societies throughout history, but never at the speed with which it is occurring in our society today.

Also, this didn't happen by accident. As we will see in the next essay, the architects of this seismic cultural shift were extremely thoughtful and intentional. Their approach was exactly what Theo Hobson's theory described. Fortunately, their strategy was thoroughly documented and widely published. We should thank them for their openness and transparency because their strategies, which worked so well, and which brought all of us to where we are today, actually provide an excellent roadmap for us, the Christian church, as we develop our own strategies for dealing with this situation going forward.

Again I want to encourage you to take heart. All is not lost. The last word on the issue has not been spoken, and the outcome is not a foregone conclusion. As time passes, societies go through cultural shifts. The changes come, they stay for a while, and then things change again. But when it's all said and done, Jesus is still on the Throne, and it is His Kingdom that remains and which continues to grow. In the long run, God always wins.

We Must Change
Our Approach

"For the people of this world are more shrewd in dealing with their own kind than are the people of the light."

Luke 16:8

In 1987 President Bill Clinton, under great pressure from Congress and from the American people, signed into law the Defense of Marriage Act (DOMA). This law affirmed that marriage is between one man and one woman. At that time the leaders of the Gay and Lesbian Agenda conceded defeat and publically lamented that their quest to legalize same-sex marriage was lost.

However shortly after that, Marshall Kirk and Hunter Madsen wrote a book entitled *After the Ball: How America Will Conquer Its Fear and Hatred of Gays in the '90s.*[18] In this book Kirk and Madsen declared that the cause was not lost at all, the Gay community simply needed a new strategy. Up to this point the movement had been unorganized, lacked focus, and they came across as militant and angry. Therefore not only were they ineffective, but they were scaring people.

The authors urged their readers to first of all, modify their speech. Gays needed to come across as kind, compassionate, soft-spoken and gentle - in short, non-threatening. Second, they should go to great lengths to portray homosexual relationships as normal and natural – no different from

---

18   Marshall Kirk and Hunter Madsen, *After the Ball: How America Will Conquer Its Fear and Hatred of Gays in the Nineties* (New York: Penguin Books, 1989)

heterosexual relationships. Then, they should work to recruit allies in the arts and media to help promote their cause. They also needed to portray themselves as victims of discrimination and unfair treatment. And finally, it was essential for them to keep promoting their message at every opportunity because if you say something often enough, eventually people begin to conclude it must be true.

The authors also taught that facts are no match for a compelling story. So they encouraged the Gay and Lesbian community to promote their cause by telling lots of heart-warming stories about same-sex families.

As we all know, their strategy worked beautifully. In only twenty-five years the situation has been almost entirely reversed. DOMA is no longer the law and same-sex marriage is now legal, celebrated, and promoted as normal and natural.

Is there a lesson in this for the Church? Sadly, yes. The Gay and Lesbian leaders have been smarter about this than we have. While they were being kind and compassionate, many of us were being cold, hard, and dogmatic. While they were telling funny and heart-warming stories, we were pounding pulpits and calling down hellfire and brimstone. While they were drawing people in with their message, we were alienating people with ours - which was the exact opposite effect that Jesus had most of the time. Jesus spoke words of truth without compromise, and yet because of His loving and winsome manner, people flocked to be near Him.

It is absolutely essential that we do not compromise doctrine. But it is equally essential that we present the truth in love and not in anger. In a gentle and kind way, we must help people to see that the Biblical way is the best way. In the next essay we will consider some ways the Church can accomplish this.

Don't Give Up

"So we must not get tired of doing good, for we will reap at the proper time if we don't give up."

Galatians 6:9

Jennifer Marshall is the Director of Domestic Policy Studies for the Heritage Foundation, which is a prominent conservative think tank. In an interview she once was asked the question: "Is same-sex marriage inevitable?" By that the interviewer meant "Is nationwide legalization of same-sex marriage inevitable? Is this a lost cause for the church?" That question was asked some years ago, and same-sex marriage is now legal nationwide, but Jennifer's response was still insightful and helpful:

"After the Roe v Wade decision in 1973, many people thought the abortion question was settled. To the contrary, the pro-life movement has grown stronger each decade, and young people today are more pro-life than their parent's generation. That's the result of sound argument and winsome engagement on the subject. The marriage question demands no less of us today." [19]

Even though same-sex marriage is now legal in the entire United States, the question is still not settled in the hearts and minds of many individuals. There will always be those who believe that marriage between people of the same sex is not the same as the marriage between a man and

---

19   Sean McDowell and John Stonestreet. *Same-Sex Marriage: A thoughtful Approach to God's Design for Marriage*, (Grand Rapids: Baker Books, 2014), p50 "An Interview With Jennifer Marshall"

a woman. There will also always be those who struggle with the issue and who aren't sure what to think. Therefore the Christian community must continue to contend for the Biblical model of marriage regardless of what the new norms of secular society might be.

As the cultural juggernaut of the Gay and Lesbian Agenda appears to be picking up speed and momentum, how should the Christian community respond? Here's a simple three step approach:

1. Know what you believe and why you believe it. It's essential for Christians to first of all know what the Bible really says about this issue. And we must also do our homework so we have at least a basic understanding of what the cultural issues are on the other side of the issue, so we can then speak intelligently about them. In Hosea 4:6 the prophet lamented that, "My people are destroyed for lack of knowledge." Let that not be true of us.

2. Advocate for Biblical principles with boldness and courage, but also with kindness and love. Speak-up! Don't be intimidated and don't allow the PC Police to silence you. Jesus commanded us to be salt and light in our world (Matthew 5:13). We will not be salt and light if we are timid and silent.

3. Don't give-up. Galatians 6:9 tells us to stand for Biblical goodness and don't give-up. Jesus is still on the throne and the church still has a responsibility to advocate for Biblical principles. Nothing is ever over until we give-up. Even if same-sex marriage is legalized nationwide (as is abortion), the battle is not over and the issue is not settled.

In the next essay we will give a little more thought to Theo Hobson's theory regarding initiating a moral revolution in a society. We will consider how the Christian community can use that same strategy to turn the cultural tide back in favor of the Biblical sexual ethic.

Just Be The Church

"For the grace of God has appeared with salvation for all people, instructing us to deny godlessness and worldly lusts and to live in a sensible, righteous, and godly way in the present age."

Titus 2:11-12

In his book *Love into Light,* author and Pastor Peter Hubbard draws on the lessons of Paul's letter to Titus. Hubbard uses that example to provide Christians in our day a roadmap for dealing with the cultural shift in sexual ethics which is occurring in our society.[20]

Hubbard explains that Titus was appointed by Paul to be the pastor of the fledging new church on the island of Crete. It was a difficult task because the culture there was extremely immoral and the people were not receptive to Biblical standards of conduct. So Paul gave Titus a simple three-step process to follow:

1. Appoint elders in every town. "This is the reason I left you in Crete ... to appoint elders in every town." (1:5-16)

2. Apply sound doctrine to every situation. "But you must say things that are consistent with sound teaching." (2:2-15)

3. Be courteous in every situation. "... be kind, always showing

---

20 Hubbard, p154

gentleness to all people." (3:1-11)

Paul's explanation to Titus helps us to understand how we are to conduct ourselves in our culture. First, as the Church, we must be a strong and confident presence in our community. Second, we are to stand firm on the clear teaching of Scripture, refusing to give-in to pressure or to compromise sound doctrine. And third, our manner is to be kind, respectful, and gentle. Ours is to be a winsome witness that draws people in rather than pushing them away.

In short, we are to simply be the church. Evangelism, along with a compelling demeanor, is the answer. The battle is not ours, it's the Lord's. We are to simply persevere and be faithful - He will take care of the outcome.

Also, history is on our side. Cultural shifts have come and cultural shifts have gone but through it all the kingdom of God has endured and continued to grow. The same will be true in our day. We just need to be faithful, bold, courageous, smart, and clever.

Civil Disobedience

"But Peter and the apostles replied: 'We must obey God rather than men.'"

Acts 5:29

The Bible is clear that Christians are to be good law-abiding citizens in whatever society they live in. The laws of the land differ greatly depending on the land that you live in. No matter, Christians are still to be the best citizens of whatever society they're part of and we are to obey the laws, whatever they are - unless those laws conflict with Biblical principles. Then we are to engage in civil disobedience. That's what Peter was saying in Acts 5:29.

Christians in the USA are increasingly finding themselves faced with the prospect of engaging in civil disobedience for the sake of Biblical principles with respect to sexual ethics and the associated cultural issues. But that disobedience always comes with a cost. Christian pharmacists have been fired for refusing to dispense abortion-inducing drugs. Christian medical students have been dismissed from medical school for declining to be trained in abortion procedures. Christian business owners have been sued for refusing to provide photography services or bake cakes for a same-sex wedding. In one city, Christian pastors were ordered to turn over to government authorities any sermons, Bible studies, and private communications with church members, that had anything to do with gay and lesbian issues or which made reference to that city's lesbian mayor. Those pastors faced the potential of going to jail for failure to comply.

This is nothing new in Christian history. It is actually rather mild compared to what other Christians in other places have endured in the past, and continue to endure today. (In China pastors aren't considered to be fully qualified or fully trained for the ministry until they've spent at least three years in prison for their faith.)

As the cultural shift in America continues, Christians can expect to experience more opposition, and perhaps even penalties, for being faithful to Biblical principles. While we aren't inviting or seeking the persecution, we should not fear it or shy away from it either. They opposed Jesus in His day, and He assured us that they will likewise oppose us in our day.

The answer for Christians today in the USA is the same as it has always been for Christians everywhere in every age – we are to faithfully stand for Biblical principles. If that means we have to take our lumps, then we take our lumps. God is faithful and He will get us through it. We have read the last chapter of the last book of the Bible and so we know how this ends. Just be faithful and trust God.

But we are not to be doormats either, and we are not to simply roll over in the face of opposition and persecution. In the next essay we will discuss some specific steps churches need to take to protect themselves as things continue to change in our society.

Protect Yourself

"I am sending you out like sheep among wolves. Therefore be as shrewd as snakes and as innocent as doves."

Matthew 10:16 (NIV)

It's a tough world out there and so Jesus instructed His followers to be smart and to protect themselves. We are to be pure and holy, innocent of wrong doing and of wrong motives, but we are not to be doormats or punching bags, allowing culture and society to unload on us or to take unfair advantage of us. Even the apostle Paul used the protections available to him as a result of being a Roman citizen (Acts 25:11)

As the moral revolution of sexual ethics continues to unfold in our nation, Christians and churches will likely find themselves increasingly at odds with society; and we will perhaps find ourselves facing the necessity of engaging in civil disobedience for the sake of Biblical principles. For years many Christian leaders have been concerned that a time is coming when the government will demand that churches accept and promote an understanding of sexuality and gender that directly opposes God's Word.

That time is here. It is already happening. In the previous essay I mentioned the case where pastors in Houston were ordered to turn over their sermons, Bible studies, and private communications with church members. Here's another example. Chai Feldblum served as a Commissioner on the Federal Equal Employment Opportunity Commission in the previous administration. He was quoted as saying,

"There can be a conflict between religious liberty and sexual liberty, but in almost all cases sexual liberty should win ..." [21]

That comes from a high ranking Federal official who had great influence over what happens in workplaces all across this country. We are already seeing the impact that kind of thinking is having on Christian businesses and ministries. Soon attempts will probably be made to apply it to churches as well.

We have all heard much talk in recent years about the constitutional guarantee of the "separation of church and state." We commonly think of it as a guarantee that the church has a right to function in the public sector, outside the walls of the church building. That is true, but the original intent of the provision was actually more focused on keeping the state out of the church. It's about preventing the state from getting inside and intruding into church affairs. We have now come to the point in this country where churches must erect strong walls of separation to keep the state out of the church. There are still legal protections that exist which we must ensure we are taking full advantage of.

The Alliance Defending Freedom is a Christian legal association which assists individual Christians, Christian business owners, and churches in defending religious freedoms. They provide guidance, resources, and legal representation. Recently they published a very helpful guidebook entitled, *Protecting Your Ministry from Sexual Orientation and Gender Identity Lawsuits.* [22] The book addresses everything from Church Constitutions and By-laws, to statements of faith, to marriage and wedding contracts, to facilities' use agreements, and much more. Every church should have a copy of this book and should modify their existing governing documents to ensure the church is fully protected under existing law.

In the final essay we will conclude our study of sexual ethics with the story of a high-profile Christian whose name you will probably recognize. This person found himself immersed in a national scandal as a result of defending Biblical principles, and he handled it very well.

---

21 https://familyfoundation.org/blog/?offset=1294772681000, 1/10/2011

22 www.adflegal.org

Shine The Light

"In the same way, let your light shine before men, so that they may see your good works and give glory to your Father in heaven."

Matthew 5:16

In the course of this study I've made reference to some books which were instrumental in shaping the thinking and establishing the strategies which have led the gay community to achieve their goals. Similarly, today the Christian community has a wealth of good literature available which is helpful and informative. But in terms of approach and strategy, two of the most helpful books I have discovered are *Love into Light* by Peter Hubbard, and *Same-Sex Marriage* by Sean McDowell and John Stonestreet. These two books provide a roadmap forward for the Christian community similar to what the other books did for the gay community.

As we conclude, I want to offer a few insights shared by Hubbard in his book and by McDowell and Stonestreet in theirs. First of all, culture is shaped, formed, and moved from the bottom up, not from the top down. Cultural elites can make suggestions and promote ideas, but it is average people like you and me who ultimately form and move culture. Our job as the Church is to model and promote healthy and happy traditional marriages. Each of our individual examples will make a difference, and collectively we can move culture and change society.

In *Love into Light* Peter Hubbard urges us to remember that gay people are in fact people. At several junctures he makes the point that we often forget that the vast majority of our fellow citizens who identify as homosexual are everyday people with jobs, hobbies, family and to-do lists. What they want may be wrong and more harmful than they know, but our tendency to overlook their humanity has hampered our ability to communicate with them effectively and to convey the love of Christ.

In that same book Hubbard also tells the story of how in 2012 Dan Cathy, the CEO of Chick-fil-A, caused a nationwide controversy when he commented to a reporter that he believes marriage is between a man and a woman only. In response, Shane Windmeyer, a well-known leader in the Gay and Lesbian community, organized a nationwide boycott of Chick-fil-A restaurants. He staged protests, "Eat-ins" and "Kiss-ins" at Chick-fil-A restaurants across the country.

Dan responded to all of this calmly and with great grace. At every opportunity and in every interview he affirmed his position without apology or compromise, but he also expressed his genuine concern for gays as people. Dan also called Shane on the phone and they spoke for over an hour. Then Dan invited Shane to be his personal guest, all expenses paid, to the Chick-fil-A college football bowl game. Shane sat with Dan in his private corporate box seats.

Later Shane wrote a magazine article entitled, "Dan Cathy and Me: My Coming Out as a Friend of Dan Cathy and Chick-fil-A." [23] In the article Shane described his encounter with Dan. He wrote that Dan shared stories of his own life and family, and he asked many questions about Shane's life and family, including about Shane's husband Tommy.

Dan and Shane ended up spending many hours together just getting to know each other and enjoying each others company. Neither of them ever changed their views about sexual ethics or gay marriage. But they did gain a new respect for each other, and they agreed that they could disagree on this issue without vilifying each other. Shane then called off the protests and the entire controversy faded away.

As we the Church move forward into this new cultural setting which is developing all around us, let us not lose sight of the fact that gays are people who are not very different from us, and we gain nothing by being unkind or insensitive. We must remember that our real battle is spiritual and the real enemy is Satan. We must resolve to simply be the Church. We must speak the truth without hesitation and without compromise, and we must love people (all people) in the Name of Jesus and in the power of His Holy Spirit

---

23 https://www.huffingtonpost.com/shane-l.../dan-cathy-chick-fil-a_b2564379.html

Afterword

As I write these final thoughts, in April 2018, the angry debate about sexual ethics in our society has cooled a bit. It has been replaced to some extent, and for the moment, by a significant escalation in tension and angry exchanges between liberals and conservatives regarding a different issue. The tension and anger is actually being expressed broadly regarding a wide variety of political and social issues, but the cause getting the most attention, at the moment, is gun control and second amendment rights. As with the debate about sexual ethics, the rhetoric on both sides is hot, heavy, and caustic.

This is not to say the debate about sexual ethics has gone away, it has not. It is simply being drowned out for the time being by the noise surrounding other issues. In time the focus will shift from gun control to something else, but the lack of civility towards those with whom we disagree, and the apparent inability to engage in reasoned and respectful discussion about our differences, continues to be a big problem.

Also, although the issue of gun control and second amendment rights is an important one (as are many of the other issues our society is contending with), it is not necessarily a Biblical issue. Sexual ethics is. That being the case, Christians must remain engaged and guarded. We dare not allow ourselves to be lulled into a sense of complacency simply because the attention has shifted to other issues for the moment.

It is my prayer that you have found the essays contained in this book to have been informative and helpful. I also pray that you will use these lessons as you strive to be salt and light in our world – boldly and courageously contending for Biblical principles, but doing so in a loving and kind way. I would love to receive feedback from you. Please contact me by visiting my website at www.JimMesereauBooks.com.

Finally, I wish to offer you the blessing Moses spoke to the nation of Israel in Numbers 6:24-26

"May the Lord bless you and protect you; may the Lord make his face shine on you and be gracious to you; may the Lord look with favor on you and give you peace."

About the Author

JIM MERSEREAU is the Pastor of Oak Hill Baptist Church in Crossville, TN. He is a retired Naval Officer and he has also served as a Family Counselor; as the Vice-President of an international humanitarian relief agency; and as the Senior Pastor of two churches in California. Jim is also the author of two previous books, Bringing it Home: A Post-Trip Devotional Guide for International and Domestic Short-Term Mission Teams, and Walking with Paul: A Journey through the Lessons of Ephesians. Jim holds a Bachelor of Arts degree in Political Science from the University of Kansas; a Master of Science degree in Instructional Technology from National University; a Master of Arts degree in Biblical Studies from the Southern California Bible College and Seminary; and a Doctor of Ministry degree from Andersonville Baptist Seminary. Jim and his wife Linda make their home in Crossville, TN. They have four adult children.

Don't Crash and Burn!

Introducing the essential debriefing tool for every short-termer beginning day one back home from the mission field. This pivotal 14-day devotional is designed to lead short-termers to prayerfully think through their mission experience, gain insight into what God was teaching, and learn how those lessons should make a difference in the practice of faith back home.

"Bringing It Home" functions intentionally as the post-field, back-home follow-up companion guide to Cindy Judge's popular best-selling pre-field devotional journal, "Before You Pack Your Bags, Prepare Your Heart."

For maximum impact in your short-term mission program, be sure that every short-termer comes back home to his/her own copy of "Bringing It Home." Add this 68-page paperback to your required reading list for every mission-bound ministry.

"Comparing your mountain-top experience "there" with being back "here" can be hard to navigate without some help. This devotional guide will help you re-enter your life at home by guiding you through the rough spots and many of the things that you wonder about after getting home."

— Cindy Judge, Author

"This is a LOT of GREAT packed into a SMALL package! Excellent for any age ... the scriptures and questions help you navigate the life-change that can be realized as God continues His great work in your life!"

— Brian Heerwagen, Author

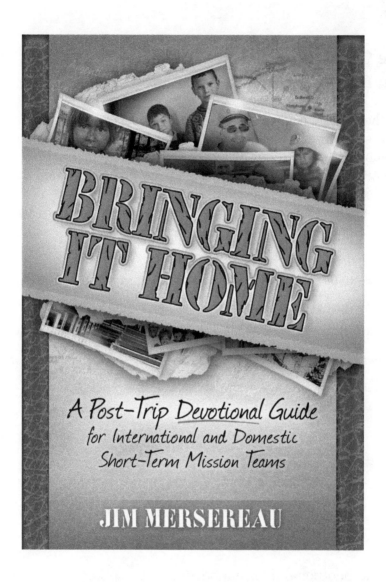

Bringing It Home is available for purchase on the author's website at
http://www.JimMersereauBooks.com, or any major retailers.

For additional information, email the author directly at
jmersereau@jimmersereaubooks.com

The Christian life is a journey through this world on our way toward our real home in heaven.

But the journey is not easy, and the situations we encounter along the way are sometimes confusing. How do we pass through this world, with all its subtle allure, devious distractions, and dangerous detours, without going astray? Through the lessons of his letter to the Ephesians Paul walks with us, serving as counselor, mentor, and guide. Along the way he offers practical advice and important life lessons which enable Christians to travel well and live victoriously.

"Walking with Paul is the best life application work on the Book of Ephesians I have read. This book will transform your spiritual walk with God in Christ. Jim has a precious gift of making solid Christian doctrine simple, but profound, as well as fun to read. I highly recommend it for a small group study."

— Candido Segarra, Author

★★★★★

―――――――――――――

Walking with Paul is available for purchase on the author's website at **http://www.JimMersereauBooks.com**, or any major retailers.

For additional information, email the author directly at
jmersereau@jimmersereaubooks.com

WALKING
WITH
PAUL

A Journey
THROUGH THE
LESSONS OF
Ephesians

JIM MERSEREAU

CPSIA information can be obtained
at www.ICGtesting.com
Printed in the USA
LVHW03s0757130718
583468LV00002B/7/P